Let Data Take The Wheel

Everything A Dealer Needs To Navigate The Data Landscape

Written By

Richie Bello

C. Mike Lewis

Copyright © 2024 Richie Bello, C. Mike Lewis

Published by Branded Expert Press

Legal Description

All Rights Reserved. No part of this publication may be reproduced in any form or by any means, including scanning, photocopying, or otherwise, without prior written permission of the copyright holder.

Disclaimer and Terms of Use: The Author and Publisher have strived to be as accurate and complete as possible in the creation of this book, notwithstanding the fact that they do not warrant or represent at any time that the contents within are accurate due to the rapidly changing nature of the Internet. While all attempts have been made to verify information provided in this publication, the Author and Publisher assume no responsibility for errors, omissions, or contrary interpretation of the subject matter herein. Any perceived slights of specific persons, doctors, or organizations are unintentional. In practical advice books, there are no guarantees of income made like anything else in life. Readers are cautioned to rely on their judgment about their circumstances to act accordingly. This book is not intended for use as a source of legal, business, accounting, medical, or financial advice. All readers are advised to seek the services of competent professionals in the legal, business, accounting, medical, and finance fields.

Dedication

All profits from this book will be donated to our U. S. Military Veterans who need hope in their lives. Suicide is a complex problem that disproportionately impacts the military community. Stop Soldier Suicide is the only national nonprofit focused solely on solving the issue of suicide among U.S. military veterans and service members.

Every dollar over the cost of publishing will be dedicated to StopSoldierSuicide.org. Let's continue to give hope to our heroes.

Preface

Unlock the Future of Automotive Sales with Big Data

In a rapidly evolving industry, the power of big data is transforming how car dealerships operate, compete, and thrive. "The Power of Big Data in the Automotive Industry" offers an in-depth exploration of the ways big data is revolutionizing the automotive sector, providing dealerships with the tools and insights needed to stay ahead in a competitive market.

Inside This Book:

Introduction to Big Data: Understand the fundamentals of big data and its unique characteristics—Volume, Velocity, And Variety—and why it matters in today's car dealership landscape.

Leveraging Customer Data: Discover how to collect, organize, and analyze customer data to unveil critical insights into demographics, preferences, and buying behaviors, driving personalized marketing strategies.

Optimizing Inventory Management: Learn how to use big data to forecast demand accurately, manage inventory efficiently, and streamline the procurement and distribution process to meet customer needs.

Enhancing the Sales Process: Explore data-driven techniques to personalize the sales experience, optimize the sales funnel, and implement effective sales tactics using cutting-edge AI and machine learning tools.

Improving Customer Retention and Loyalty: Uncover strategies to enhance customer retention through targeted efforts, customer lifetime value analysis, and exceptional post-sale experiences.

Predictive Analytics for Future Sales: Apply predictive analytics to anticipate customer needs, identify emerging market trends, and prepare for the future of car sales, including the impact of autonomous vehicles.

Building a Data-Driven Culture: Learn how to foster a data-centric mindset within your organization, overcome resistance to change, and develop the skills and infrastructure necessary for data-driven decision-making.

IoT integration Real-World Case Studies: Gain insights from detailed case studies of dealerships that have successfully harnessed big data, showcasing best practices and lessons from industry leaders.

A Vision for the Future: The transformative potential of big data and encouraging continuous learning and adaptation to stay at the forefront of the automotive industry.

Whether you are a dealership owner, manager, or industry professional, this book provides a comprehensive guide to leveraging big data for strategic advantage, driving growth, and delivering exceptional customer experiences. Embrace the power of big data and unlock new opportunities in the ever-evolving automotive market.

Table of Contents

Chapter 1
The Power of Big Data in the Automotive Industry

Chapter 2
Leveraging Customer Data

Chapter 3
Optimizing Inventory Management

Chapter 4
Enhancing the Sales Process

Chapter 5
Improving Customer Retention and Loyalty

Chapter 6
Predictive Analytics and the Future of Car Sales

Chapter 7
Implementing a Data-Driven Culture

Chapter 8
Case Studies and Best Practices

Chapter 9
Summarizing the Key Benefits of Using Big Data in Car Sales

About the Authors
Richie Bello

C. Mike Lewis

Chapter 1

The Power of Big Data in the Automotive Industry

In the rapidly evolving landscape of the 21st century, few industries have undergone as dramatic a transformation as the automotive sector. Once dominated by mechanical innovation and manufacturing prowess, the industry now finds itself at the forefront of a digital revolution. At the heart of this seismic shift lies an intangible and immensely powerful force: data. With its complex supply chains, intricate consumer relationships, and high-stakes transactions, the automotive industry has become a fertile ground for applying big data analytics. This chapter explores the transformative potential of big data in the automotive industry, focusing on its impact on car dealerships and sales processes.

Introduction to Big Data and Its Transformative Potential

The digital transformation sweeping through the automotive industry is not merely a matter of adopting new technologies; it represents a fundamental reimagining of how vehicles are designed, manufactured, sold, and operated. From the factory floor to the showroom, from the driver's seat to the mechanic's garage, data is being generated, collected, and analyzed at an unprecedented scale. This deluge of information is reshaping every facet of the automotive value chain, offering insights that were once unimaginable and unlocking new avenues for innovation and efficiency.

In the broader context of modern economies, data has emerged as a critical resource, often likened to oil in its value and transformative potential. This analogy is particularly apt in sectors characterized by high levels of consumer interaction and transaction volumes, such as the automotive industry. Just as oil fueled the industrial revolutions of the past, data is powering the digital revolution of today. For car manufacturers and dealerships, the ability to harness this resource effectively can mean the difference between leading the pack and being left in the dust.

The automotive industry's embrace of big data is driven by several factors:

1. Consumer Expectations: Today's car buyers are more informed and demanding than ever before. They expect personalized experiences, tailored recommendations, and seamless interactions across multiple channels. Big data enables companies to meet these expectations by providing deep insights into consumer preferences and behaviors.

2. Competitive Pressures: In a market where margins are often tight, and competition is fierce, the insights provided by big data can offer a crucial edge. From optimizing inventory management to precision marketing, data-driven strategies are becoming essential for survival and success.

3. Technological Advancements: The increasing sophistication of data collection and analysis tools, coupled with the growing ubiquity of connected devices, has made it possible to gather and process vast amounts of data in real-time. This technological leap has opened up new possibilities for innovation and optimization throughout the automotive value chain.

4. Regulatory Compliance: As governments worldwide implement stricter emissions standards and safety regulations, automakers and dealers must rely on data to ensure compliance and adapt their strategies accordingly.

Defining Big Data and Its Key Characteristics

To fully appreciate the impact of big data on the automotive industry, it's essential to understand what exactly we mean by the term. While there is no universally accepted definition, big data is generally characterized by the "Three V's": Volume, Velocity, and Variety. Let's explore each of these characteristics in the context of the automotive industry:

1. Volume:

The sheer quantity of data generated in the automotive sector is staggering. Consider the following sources:

- Connected Cars: Modern vehicles are essentially computers on wheels, equipped with dozens of sensors that continuously generate data on everything from engine performance to driver behavior.
- Manufacturing Processes: Advanced factories use IoT devices to monitor every aspect of the production line, generating terabytes of data daily.
- Customer Interactions: From website visits to test drives, from service appointments to social media engagement, every touchpoint with a customer generates valuable data.
- Market and Economic Indicators: External data sources, such as economic trends, weather patterns, and demographic shifts, also contribute to the volume of data relevant to the automotive industry.

For a large car dealership or manufacturer, the volume of data being processed can easily reach petabytes (millions of gigabytes) per year.

2. Velocity:

In the fast-paced world of automotive sales and manufacturing, the speed at which data is generated and needs to be processed is crucial. Examples include:

- ➤ Real-time Vehicle Diagnostics: Connected cars can transmit performance data in real-time, allowing for predictive maintenance and rapid response to potential issues.
- ➤ Dynamic Pricing Models: Dealerships can adjust prices in real-time based on market demand, competitor actions, and inventory levels.
- ➤ Supply Chain Management: Real-time data on parts availability, shipping delays, and production schedules allows for agile decision-making in the complex automotive supply chain.
- ➤ Customer Service: Instant access to customer history and preferences enables personalized service at every interaction.

The ability to process and act on this high-velocity data can be a significant competitive advantage in the automotive industry.

3. Variety:

The automotive industry deals with an incredibly diverse range of data types, including:

- ➤ Structured Data: Traditional databases containing customer information, sales records, and inventory details.
- ➤ Unstructured Data: Text from customer reviews, social media posts, and service reports.
- ➤ Semi-structured Data: Log files from vehicles and manufacturing equipment.
- ➤ Multimedia Data: Images and videos from security cameras, marketing materials, and vehicle inspections.
- ➤ Geospatial Data: GPS data from test drives, delivery routes, and customer locations.

The ability to integrate and analyze these diverse data types is crucial for gaining a comprehensive understanding of the business and its customers.

In addition to these three core characteristics, two additional "V's" are often considered when discussing big data, particularly in the context of car sales:

4. Veracity:

This refers to the reliability and accuracy of the data. In the automotive industry, where decisions can have significant financial and safety implications, ensuring data quality is paramount. Examples of challenges related to data veracity include:

- Inconsistent Customer Information: Customers may provide different information across various touchpoints, leading to conflicting records.
- Sensor Malfunctions: Faulty sensors in vehicles or manufacturing equipment can produce erroneous data.
- Human Error: Mistakes in data entry or interpretation can lead to flawed analyses.

Dealerships and manufacturers must implement robust data governance practices and validation processes to maintain high levels of data veracity.

5. Value:

Ultimately, the true measure of big data's importance lies in the value it creates. In the automotive industry, this value can take many forms:

- Improved Customer Experiences: By leveraging data to understand customer preferences and behaviors, dealerships can offer personalized services that enhance satisfaction and loyalty.
- Optimized Operations: Data-driven insights can lead to more efficient inventory management, reduced waste in manufacturing processes, and streamlined supply chains.

> Innovation: Analysis of usage patterns and customer feedback can inform product development, leading to vehicles that better meet market demands.
> Risk Management: Predictive analytics can help identify potential quality issues or market risks before they become major issues.

The ability to extract actionable insights from big data and translate them into tangible business value is what separates successful automotive companies from their competitors.

Importance of Big Data in the Modern Car Dealership Landscape

The adoption of big data analytics in the automotive industry is not merely a trend; it's a competitive necessity. Car dealerships, in particular, face a range of pressures that make the effective use of data crucial for survival and success:

1. Changing Consumer Behavior: Today's car buyers often begin their journey online, researching options and comparing prices before ever setting foot in a dealership. Big data allows dealers to track these digital touchpoints and engage with potential customers at the right moment with the right message.

2. Margin Pressure: With information readily available online, price competition has intensified, squeezing dealership margins. Data-driven strategies for inventory management, pricing, and upselling are essential for maintaining profitability.

3. Shift to Electric and Autonomous Vehicles: As the industry moves towards electric and autonomous vehicles, dealerships need to adapt their sales and service models. Data analytics can help predict market trends and guide the transition to new technologies.

4. Increased Competition: Not only are dealerships competing with each other, but they also face competition from direct-to-consumer

sales models and online marketplaces. Big data can provide the insights needed to differentiate and add value in this crowded marketplace.

Case Studies: Big Data in Action

To illustrate the transformative power of big data in the automotive sales landscape, let's examine a few case studies:

1. Inventory Optimization at AutoNation:

AutoNation, the largest automotive retailer in the United States, implemented a big data analytics platform to optimize its inventory across its network of dealerships. By analyzing historical sales data, local market trends, and even weather patterns, AutoNation was able to:

- Reduce overall inventory levels by 10% without impacting sales
- Increase the turnover rate of vehicles on the lot
- Improve the mix of vehicles to better match local demand

The result was a significant improvement in inventory efficiency and a reduction in carrying costs.

2. Personalized Marketing at BMW:

BMW leveraged its customer data to create highly targeted marketing campaigns. By analyzing data from test drives, service appointments, and online interactions, BMW was able to:

- Create detailed customer segments based on preferences and behaviors
- Develop personalized offers and content for each segment
- Increase conversion rates on marketing campaigns by over 30%

This data-driven approach not only improved the effectiveness of BMW's marketing efforts but also enhanced the customer experience by providing more relevant and timely communications.

3. Predictive Maintenance at Tesla:

Tesla's connected vehicles generate vast amounts of data on vehicle performance and usage. By analyzing this data in real-time, Tesla has been able to:

- Predict potential vehicle issues before they occur
- Schedule preventive maintenance proactively
- Push software updates to improve vehicle performance and features

This approach has not only improved customer satisfaction but has also reduced warranty costs and strengthened Tesla's brand reputation for innovation and reliability.

These case studies demonstrate the wide-ranging impact of big data on various aspects of automotive sales and service. From optimizing inventory and marketing to enhancing product quality and customer service, the applications of big data in the automotive industry are vast and continually evolving.

The power of big data in the automotive industry is undeniable. As we've explored in this chapter, the volume, velocity, variety, veracity, and value of data are reshaping every aspect of the automotive value chain. For car dealerships, the ability to harness this data effectively is no longer a luxury—it's a necessity for survival and success in an increasingly competitive and digitally-driven marketplace.

As we move forward, the role of big data in the automotive industry will only grow in importance. The advent of autonomous vehicles, the continued growth of electric cars, and the increasing connectivity of vehicles will generate even more data, offering new opportunities for innovation and optimization. Dealerships and manufacturers that invest in developing their data analytics capabilities now will be well-positioned to lead the industry in the years to come.

In the following chapters, we will delve deeper into specific applications of big data in automotive sales, exploring topics such as predictive analytics for lead scoring, dynamic pricing strategies, and the use of artificial intelligence in customer service. We will also address the challenges and ethical considerations that come with the use of big data, including data privacy concerns and the need for transparent and responsible data practices.

The journey of digital transformation in the automotive industry is just beginning, and big data is the fuel that will power this revolution. As we stand on the brink of this new era, one thing is clear: the future of automotive sales will be data-driven, customer-centric, and more innovative than ever before.

Chapter 2

Leveraging Customer Data

In the digital age, data has become the lifeblood of successful businesses, and the automotive industry is no exception. As we explored in the previous chapter, the sheer volume and variety of data available to car dealerships and manufacturers are staggering. However, the true power of this data lies not in its quantity but in how effectively it can be leveraged to understand and serve customers better. This chapter delves into the intricate process of collecting, organizing, and analyzing customer data to develop personalized marketing strategies that drive sales and foster long-term customer relationships.

Collecting and Organizing Customer Data from Various Sources

The first step in leveraging customer data is to gather it from a multitude of sources and organize it into a coherent, usable format. In the automotive industry, customer data comes from a diverse array of touchpoints, each offering unique insights into customer behavior, preferences, and needs.

1. Online Interactions:

In today's digital-first world, a significant portion of the car-buying journey happens online. Key sources of online customer data include:

- ✓ Website Visits: Tracking pages viewed, time spent on each page, and the customer's journey through the site can provide insights into their interests and intentions.
- ✓ Search Queries: Understanding what customers are searching for can help dealerships tailor their inventory and marketing messages.
- ✓ Social Media Interactions: Likes, shares, comments, and direct

messages on platforms like Facebook, Instagram, and Twitter offer a wealth of information about customer preferences and sentiments.
- ✓ Email Interactions: Open rates, click-through rates, and responses to email campaigns can indicate customer engagement levels and interests.

Techniques for integrating this online data often involve the use of web analytics tools, social media listening platforms, and customer relationship management (CRM) systems that can capture and centralize digital interactions.

2. Showroom Visits:

While online interactions are crucial, the physical dealership remains a vital touchpoint. Data from showroom visits can include:

- ✓ Test Drive Information: Which models are most popular for test drives? How does test drive behavior correlate with purchase decisions?
- ✓ Salesperson Interactions: Notes from conversations with customers can provide valuable qualitative data about their needs and preferences.
- ✓ Footfall Analytics: Understanding peak visiting hours, dwell time in different areas of the showroom, and customer flow can help optimize the in-person experience.

Integrating this data often requires a combination of CRM systems, where salespeople can log interactions, and more advanced technologies like IoT sensors for tracking customer movement within the dealership.

3. Maintenance Records:

Service and maintenance data is a vast goldmine of information about customer behavior and vehicle performance:

- ✓ Service History: Frequency of visits, types of services requested, and spending patterns can indicate customer loyalty and vehicle preferences.
- ✓ Vehicle Performance Data: Information gathered during service visits can provide insights into how different models perform over time, informing both product development and sales strategies.

Integrating maintenance data typically involves connecting dealership management systems with CRM platforms to create a holistic view of the customer's relationship with their vehicle.

4. Third-Party Sources:

External data can provide valuable context and augment the dealership's own data:

- ✓ Credit Reports: Understanding a customer's financial situation can help tailor financing offers.
- ✓ Demographic Data: Information about income levels, family size, and lifestyle in different geographic areas can inform inventory decisions and marketing strategies.
- ✓ Market Trends: Data on broader automotive industry trends can help dealerships anticipate and prepare for shifts in customer preferences.

Integrating third-party data often involves partnerships with data providers and the use of data management platforms (DMPs) that can combine proprietary and third-party data.

The Importance of Data Quality and Cleaning

While collecting data from various sources is crucial, the quality of this data is equally important. Poor data quality can lead to flawed analyses and misguided decisions. Some key considerations in maintaining data quality include:

1. Data Cleansing: Regularly auditing and cleaning data to remove duplicates, correct errors, and standardize formats is essential. This process often involves both automated tools and manual review.

2. Data Validation: Implementing checks to ensure data accuracy at the point of entry can significantly reduce errors. For example, using address verification tools when customers input their information.

3. Data Governance: Establishing clear policies and procedures for data management, including who can access and modify data, helps maintain data integrity over time.

4. Data Integration: Ensuring that data from different sources is properly integrated and reconciled is crucial for building a reliable, comprehensive customer database.

5. Continuous Monitoring: Regularly assessing data quality metrics and addressing issues as they arise helps maintain the reliability of the database over time.

Investing in data quality may seem like a tedious and unglamorous task, but it's the foundation upon which all subsequent data analysis and strategy development rests. As the saying goes, "garbage in, garbage out" – no amount of sophisticated analysis can compensate for poor-quality data.

Analyzing Customer Demographics, Preferences, and Buying Behavior

With a robust, high-quality customer database in place, dealerships can begin the process of extracting meaningful insights. This analysis typically involves two key components: customer segmentation and predictive modeling.

Customer Segmentation

Segmentation involves dividing the customer base into distinct groups based on shared characteristics. In the automotive industry, relevant segmentation criteria might include:

1. Demographic Factors:

- Age
- Income
- Family size
- Occupation
- Education level

2. Geographic Factors:

- Urban/suburban/rural location
- Climate conditions (relevant for vehicle features like all-wheel drive)
- Proximity to dealership

3. Psychographic Factors:

- Lifestyle (e.g., outdoors enthusiast, tech-savvy professional)
- Values (e.g., environmental consciousness, luxury orientation)
- Personality traits

4. Behavioral Factors:

- Previous purchase history
- Service record
- Interaction with marketing materials
- Loyalty program participation

5. Vehicle Preference Factors:

- Preferred vehicle type (sedan, SUV, truck, etc.)
- New vs. used preference

- Brand loyalty

Effective segmentation allows dealerships to tailor their approaches to different customer groups, optimizing everything from inventory management to marketing messages.

Predictive Modeling

While segmentation provides a snapshot of the customer base, predictive modeling uses historical data to forecast future behavior. In the automotive industry, predictive models can be used for various purposes:

1. Lead Scoring: Predicting which potential customers are most likely to make a purchase, allowing sales teams to prioritize their efforts.

2. Churn Prediction: Identifying customers who are at risk of switching to a different brand or dealership, enabling proactive retention efforts.

3. Lifetime Value Prediction: Estimating the total value a customer is likely to bring to the dealership over their lifetime, informing customer acquisition and retention strategies.

4. Next Best Offer: Predicting which products or services a customer is most likely to be interested in next, enabling personalized recommendations.

These predictive models often employ advanced statistical techniques and machine learning algorithms. Some common approaches include:

- Logistic Regression: Useful for binary outcomes (e.g., will a customer buy or not?)
- Decision Trees: Provide easily interpretable rules for classifying customers
- Random Forests: Combine multiple decision trees for improved accuracy

- Gradient Boosting Machines: Often provide state-of-the-art performance for many prediction tasks
- Neural Networks: Can capture complex, non-linear relationships in the data

The choice of model depends on the specific prediction task, the nature of the available data, and the desired balance between model accuracy and interpretability.

Developing Personalized Marketing Strategies Based on Customer Insights

The ultimate goal of collecting and analyzing customer data is to inform more effective, personalized marketing strategies. By understanding customer segments and leveraging predictive models, dealerships can craft targeted campaigns that speak directly to each customer's needs and preferences.

Crafting Targeted Marketing Campaigns

Personalized marketing in the automotive industry can take many forms:

1. Customized Email Campaigns: Tailoring email content based on the customer's interests, previous interactions, and predicted needs. For example, sending information about family-friendly SUVs to customers who recently had a child.

2. Dynamic Website Content: Adjusting the dealership's website to highlight vehicles and offers most relevant to each visitor based on their browsing history and known preferences.

3. Personalized Social Media Advertising: Using customer data to create highly targeted ad campaigns on platforms like Facebook and Instagram, showing specific vehicle models to users most likely to be interested in them.

4. Customized Direct Mail: While often considered old-fashioned, personalized direct mail can still be effective, especially when informed by rich customer data.

5. Tailored In-Dealership Experiences: Using customer data to prepare personalized showroom experiences, with sales staff briefed on the customer's preferences and history before they arrive.

6. Personalized Service Reminders: Sending service reminders that take into account the customer's typical usage patterns and previous service history.

Examples of Successful Personalized Marketing Initiatives

To illustrate the power of data-driven, personalized marketing in the automotive industry, let's examine a few real-world examples:

1. BMW's "The Zero Project":

BMW launched a highly personalized campaign targeting potential electric vehicle buyers. By analyzing customer data, they identified individuals who had shown interest in electric vehicles but hadn't made a purchase. They created personalized videos for each potential customer, showcasing how a BMW electric vehicle would fit into their daily life based on their location, driving habits, and lifestyle data. The campaign resulted in a 30% increase in EV test drives and a significant boost in sales.

2. Toyota's Predictive Maintenance Alerts:

Toyota used data from connected vehicles to predict when customers would need maintenance services. By sending personalized, timely reminders based on actual vehicle usage rather than just mileage, they saw a 20% increase in service appointments and improved customer satisfaction scores.

3. CarMax's Omnichannel Personalization:

CarMax leveraged its customer data to create a seamless, personalized experience across online and in-store channels. By tracking customer interactions on their website and mobile app, they were able to provide sales associates with detailed information about a customer's interests and browsing history when they visited a physical location. This approach led to a 15% increase in conversion rates.

4. Audi's Virtual Reality Showroom:

Audi combined customer preference data with virtual reality technology to create personalized virtual showroom experiences. Customers could configure their ideal Audi in a VR environment, with the system suggesting options based on their known preferences and previous interactions. This innovative approach led to a 60% increase in optional feature sales.

5. Ford's "Built for You" Campaign:

Ford used customer data to create highly targeted social media ads showcasing vehicle features that aligned with each customer's interests and needs. For example, outdoor enthusiasts saw ads highlighting off-road capabilities, while urban dwellers saw ads focusing on parking assist features. This personalized approach resulted in a 24% increase in ad engagement rates.

These examples demonstrate the power of leveraging customer data to create marketing initiatives that resonate on a personal level. By speaking directly to each customer's unique needs and preferences, automotive companies can significantly improve the effectiveness of their marketing efforts.

Challenges and Ethical Considerations

While the potential of personalized marketing based on customer data is enormous, it's important to acknowledge the challenges and ethical considerations that come with this approach:

1. Data Privacy: With regulations like GDPR and CCPA, ensuring compliance with data privacy laws is crucial. Dealerships must be transparent about data collection and usage and obtain proper consent from customers.

2. Data Security: Protecting customer data from breaches is not just a legal requirement but also essential for maintaining customer trust.

3. Avoiding "Creepy" Marketing: There's a fine line between personalization and invasion of privacy. Marketing that feels too intrusive can backfire, alienating customers instead of engaging them.

4. Algorithmic Bias: Predictive models can sometimes perpetuate or amplify existing biases in the data. It's important to regularly audit these models for fairness and adjust as necessary.

5. Balancing Personalization and Choice: While personalization can enhance the customer experience, it's important not to limit customer choices based on predicted preferences. Customers should always have the option to explore beyond what the data suggests they might like.

Leveraging customer data effectively has become a crucial competency for success in the modern automotive industry. By collecting and organizing data from various sources, analyzing it to understand customer demographics, preferences, and buying behavior, and using these insights to develop personalized marketing strategies, dealerships can create more engaging, relevant experiences for their customers.

The examples we've explored demonstrate the tangible benefits of this approach, from increased sales and improved customer satisfaction to more efficient marketing spend. However, as we've also discussed, this power comes with responsibility. Dealerships must navigate the complex landscape of data privacy, security, and ethics to ensure that their use of customer data enhances, rather than detracts from, the customer relationship.

As we move forward, the role of data in shaping the customer experience will only grow. The dealerships that can master the art and science of data-driven personalization while maintaining ethical standards and customer trust will be well-positioned to thrive in the increasingly competitive automotive marketplace.

In the next chapter, we will explore how these data-driven insights can be applied beyond marketing, looking at how they can inform inventory management, pricing strategies, and even product development in the automotive industry.

Chapter 3

Optimizing Inventory Management

In the fast-paced world of automotive retail, effective inventory management can mean the difference between thriving and merely surviving. With the advent of big data and advanced analytics, dealerships now have unprecedented tools at their disposal to optimize their inventory strategies. This chapter explores how dealerships can leverage these powerful technologies to forecast demand, optimize inventory levels, identify popular vehicle configurations, and streamline their procurement and distribution processes.

Utilizing Big Data to Forecast Demand and Optimize Inventory Levels

The ability to accurately predict future demand is a cornerstone of effective inventory management. In the automotive industry, where each unit represents a significant investment and carrying costs can quickly accumulate, the importance of precise forecasting cannot be overstated. Big data and predictive analytics have revolutionized this aspect of dealership operations, allowing for more accurate, granular, and dynamic demand forecasts.

Introduction to Predictive Analytics Techniques for Demand Forecasting

Predictive analytics in demand forecasting typically involves the use of historical data, current market conditions, and external factors to project future sales. Some key techniques used in the automotive industry include:

1. Time Series Analysis: This method examines historical sales data to identify patterns and trends. It's particularly useful for

identifying seasonality in car sales, such as increased demand for convertibles in summer or SUVs in winter.
2. Regression Analysis: This statistical method helps identify the relationships between various factors (like economic indicators, marketing spending, or competitor actions) and sales volumes. For example, it might reveal how changes in local employment rates affect luxury car sales.
3. Machine Learning Algorithms: Advanced techniques like neural networks and random forests can uncover complex, non-linear relationships in the data that simpler methods might miss. These can be particularly useful for predicting demand for new models or in rapidly changing market conditions.
4. Bayesian Forecasting: This approach allows for the incorporation of expert knowledge and subjective judgments into the forecasting process, which can be valuable when dealing with unprecedented situations or launching new products.
5. Ensemble Methods: Combining multiple forecasting techniques often leads to more robust predictions, as it can balance out the weaknesses of individual methods.

Implementing these techniques requires not just sophisticated software but also a deep understanding of the local market and the broader automotive industry. Successful dealerships often combine automated forecasting systems with human expertise to achieve the best results.

Balancing Inventory Levels

Once a demand forecast is in place, the next challenge is to translate this into optimal inventory levels. The goal is to have enough vehicles on hand to meet customer demand without tying up excessive capital in unsold inventory. This balancing act involves several considerations:

1. **Lead Times:** Understanding the time it takes to procure vehicles from manufacturers or other sources is crucial. Longer lead times generally necessitate higher inventory levels to buffer against uncertainty.
2. **Carrying Costs:** Each vehicle on the lot represents tied-up capital and incurs ongoing costs (e.g., financing, insurance, depreciation). These costs must be weighed against the potential lost sales from stockouts.
3. **Model Mix:** Different models may have different optimal inventory levels based on their sales velocity, profit margins, and strategic importance.
4. **Seasonality:** Inventory strategies often need to account for predictable fluctuations in demand throughout the year.
5. **Market Position:** A dealership's competitive strategy (e.g., always having a wide selection vs. focusing on fast turnover) will influence its approach to inventory management.

Advanced inventory optimization systems use these factors, along with demand forecasts, to recommend optimal stock levels for each model and trim level. These systems often employ techniques from operations research, such as multi-echelon inventory optimization models, to balance the competing objectives of minimizing costs and maximizing service levels.

Case Study: AutoNation's Inventory Optimization

AutoNation, the largest automotive retailer in the United States, provides an excellent example of how big data can transform inventory management. In 2016, the company implemented a new inventory management system that leveraged predictive analytics to optimize stock levels across its network of dealerships.

The system analyzed historical sales data, local market conditions, and broader economic indicators to forecast demand for each model at each location. It then used this information to recommend inventory levels and facilitate the transfer of vehicles between dealerships to match supply with demand.

The results were impressive:

- Inventory turnover increased by 17%
- The average time vehicles spent on lots decreased from 66 days to 53 days
- Profits per vehicle sold increased by 11%

This case demonstrates how effective use of big data in inventory management can lead to significant improvements in operational efficiency and profitability.

Identifying Popular Models, Trims, and Features Based on Customer Trends

In addition to optimizing overall inventory levels, big data analytics can provide valuable insights into which specific vehicle configurations are most popular with customers. This granular level of understanding allows dealerships to stock the right mix of vehicles to meet customer preferences.

Analysis of Sales Data

By analyzing historical sales data, dealerships can identify patterns in customer preferences for various models, trims, and features. This analysis can reveal:

1. Popular Color Combinations: Understanding color preferences can help dealerships stock vehicles that are more likely to sell quickly.

2. In-Demand Features: Identifying which optional features (e.g., sunroofs, premium sound systems, advanced driver assistance systems) are most popular can inform decisions about which configurations to stock.
3. Trim Level Preferences: Understanding which trim levels sell best for each model can help optimize the mix of base, mid-range, and high-end configurations on the lot.
4. Seasonal Trends: Some features or models may be more popular at different times of the year. For example, all-wheel drive vehicles might see increased demand in winter months in certain regions.
5. Regional Variations: Preferences can vary significantly by geographic area. A dealership in a rural area might see higher demand for trucks and SUVs, while an urban dealership might sell more compact cars and electric vehicles.

Advanced analytics techniques like association rule mining can be particularly useful for identifying which features tend to be purchased together, allowing dealerships to stock vehicles with the most appealing combinations of options.

Real-Time Adjustments

One of the key advantages of big data systems is the ability to make real-time adjustments based on current sales trends. This might involve:

1. Dynamic Reordering: Automatically adjusting order quantities based on current sales velocity and projected demand.
2. Inventory Reallocation: Facilitating the transfer of vehicles between dealerships in a network to match local demand patterns.

3. **Pricing Adjustments:** Modifying prices on slow-moving inventory to accelerate sales and maintain optimal stock levels.
4. **Marketing Focus:** Aligning marketing efforts with current inventory to promote vehicles that are in stock and ready for immediate delivery.

Case Study: CarMax's Data-Driven Inventory Management

CarMax, the largest used-car retailer in the United States, provides an excellent example of using data to optimize inventory mix. The company analyzes millions of data points from its nationwide network of stores to understand which vehicles are most likely to sell in each location.

Their system considers factors such as local market conditions, historical sales data, vehicle conditions, and even current events that might impact demand. For example, they might increase the stock of fuel-efficient vehicles in an area experiencing rising gas prices.

This data-driven approach has allowed CarMax to:

- Reduce the average time to sell a vehicle by 25%
- Increase inventory turnover by 30%
- Improve customer satisfaction by ensuring a wide selection of in-demand vehicles at each location.

Streamlining the Procurement and Distribution of Vehicles

Effective inventory management extends beyond just deciding what to stock. It also involves optimizing how vehicles are procured and distributed. Big data analytics can play a crucial role in improving these processes.

Leveraging Data Analytics for Efficient Supply Chain Management

In the automotive retail context, supply chain management primarily involves the flow of vehicles from manufacturers or auction houses to dealerships and sometimes between dealerships in a network. Big data can enhance this process in several ways:

1. Optimized Ordering: Predictive analytics can help dealerships place orders with manufacturers that more accurately reflect future demand, reducing both overstock and stockout situations.
2. Efficient Auction Bidding: For used car dealerships, data analytics can inform bidding strategies at auctions, helping buyers quickly identify vehicles that are likely to sell well in their local market.
3. Transportation Optimization: Route optimization algorithms can reduce transportation costs and delivery times when moving vehicles between locations.
4. Predictive Maintenance: For dealerships that manage their own delivery fleets, predictive maintenance based on vehicle telematics data can reduce downtime and extend vehicle life.
5. Supplier Performance Analysis: Data analytics can help dealerships evaluate the performance of their suppliers (whether manufacturers or auction houses) in terms of delivery times, vehicle quality, and other key metrics.
6. Inventory Balancing: For dealership groups with multiple locations, analytics can facilitate the optimal distribution of vehicles across the network to match local demand patterns.

Case Study: Improved Turnaround Times and Cost Reduction

Let's consider a hypothetical case study of a mid-sized dealership group, "AutoPro Motors," with 20 locations across the Midwest United States.

Before implementing a data-driven supply chain management system, AutoPro Motors faced several challenges:

- High carrying costs due to excess inventory at some locations
- Lost sales due to stockouts of popular models at other locations
- High transportation costs from frequent inter-dealership transfers
- Slow response to changing market conditions

AutoPro Motors implemented a new supply chain management system that leveraged big data analytics. The system included the following features:

1. Centralized Inventory Visibility: Real-time data on inventory levels and sales at all locations.
2. Predictive Demand Forecasting: Machine learning models that predict demand for each model at each location based on historical data, local economic indicators, and current trends.
3. Automated Reordering: The system could automatically generate order recommendations for each dealership based on projected demand and current inventory levels.
4. Optimized Vehicle Distribution: When new vehicles arrive from manufacturers, the system would recommend the optimal distribution across the dealership network.
5. Intelligent Transfer Recommendations: The system could suggest inter-dealership transfers to balance inventory and meet customer demand.
6. Transportation Optimization: A route optimization algorithm to minimize costs when transferring vehicles between locations.

The results after one year of implementation were significant:

- Inventory carrying costs decreased by 15% due to better-aligned stock levels

- Lost sales due to stockouts decreased by 25%
- Transportation costs for inter-dealership transfers decreased by 20%
- The average time to fulfill a customer order for a specific vehicle configuration decreased from 10 days to 6 days
- Overall profitability increased by 8% due to better inventory turnover and reduced costs

This case study illustrates how a data-driven approach to supply chain management can lead to significant improvements in efficiency and profitability for automotive dealerships.

Challenges and Considerations

While the benefits of using big data for inventory management are clear, there are also challenges that dealerships must navigate:

1. Data Quality: The effectiveness of any data-driven system is only as good as the data it's based on. Ensuring data accuracy and consistency across all systems is crucial.
2. Integration Complexity: Implementing these systems often requires integrating data from multiple sources (e.g., DMS, CRM, manufacturer systems), which can be technically challenging.
3. Change Management: Moving to a data-driven inventory management approach often requires significant changes in processes and mindsets. Effective change management is crucial for successful implementation.
4. Balancing Automation and Human Judgment: While data-driven systems can provide valuable insights, it's important to combine these with human expertise and local market knowledge.

5. Handling Exceptions: No predictive system is perfect, and there will always be unexpected events (e.g., sudden changes in gas prices and new competitor actions) that require manual intervention.
6. Continuous Improvement: The automotive market is constantly evolving, so inventory management systems need to be regularly updated and refined to maintain their effectiveness.

The application of big data analytics to inventory management represents a significant opportunity for automotive dealerships to improve their operations, reduce costs, and better serve their customers. By leveraging advanced forecasting techniques, dealerships can optimize their inventory levels, ensuring they have the right vehicles in stock to meet customer demand without tying up excessive capital.

Moreover, the ability to analyze sales trends at a granular level allows dealerships to stock the specific models, trims, and features that are most popular in their local market. This not only improves inventory turnover but also enhances the customer experience by increasing the likelihood that shoppers will find exactly what they're looking for on the lot.

Finally, by extending these data-driven approaches to the entire supply chain, dealerships can streamline their procurement and distribution processes, further reducing costs and improving responsiveness to market changes.

As we move forward, the role of big data in inventory management will only grow more significant. Dealerships that can effectively harness these technologies will be well-positioned to thrive in an increasingly competitive and fast-paced automotive retail landscape.

In the next chapter, we will explore how big data is transforming another crucial aspect of automotive retail: pricing strategies. We'll examine how dealerships can use data analytics to optimize their pricing to maximize profitability while remaining competitive in their local markets.

Chapter 4

Enhancing the Sales Process

In the ever-evolving landscape of automotive retail, the sales process has undergone a significant transformation. Gone are the days of one-size-fits-all sales pitches and intuition-based tactics. Today's successful dealerships are leveraging the power of data to create personalized, efficient, and effective sales processes. This chapter explores how big data and advanced analytics are revolutionizing the way cars are sold, from the initial customer interaction to the final handshake.

Leveraging Customer Data to Personalize the Sales Experience

The cornerstone of modern sales strategies is personalization. By utilizing the wealth of customer data available, dealerships can create tailored experiences that resonate with individual buyers, increasing the likelihood of a successful sale.

Examples of Personalized Sales Approaches

1. Customized Vehicle Recommendations:

By analyzing a customer's browsing history on the dealership website, previous purchases, and demographic information, sales representatives can suggest vehicles that align with the customer's preferences before they even step foot in the showroom.

Example: John, a 35-year-old father of two, has been browsing SUVs on the dealership's website. When he visits the showroom, the sales representative is prepared with information on family-friendly SUVs with high safety ratings and ample cargo space.

2. Personalized Test Drive Routes:

Using data on a customer's typical driving habits and preferences, many

dealerships can design test drive routes that showcase the vehicle's relevant features.

Example: Sarah, who has a long daily commute, is offered a test drive route that includes both highway driving and stop-and-go traffic, allowing her to experience the vehicle's fuel efficiency and comfort in relevant conditions.

3. Tailored Financial Offerings:

By integrating credit score data and purchase history, sales representatives can present financing options that are most likely to be approved and appealing to the customer.

Example: Based on Mark's excellent credit score and preference for low monthly payments, the sales rep presents a lease option with a low down payment and competitive monthly rate.

4. Relevant Feature Highlighting:

Analysis of a customer's lifestyle data can inform which vehicle features to emphasize during the sales presentation.

Example: Emma, an avid camper, according to her social media activity, is shown how the roof rack system and all-wheel drive capabilities of an SUV can enhance her outdoor adventures.

5. Personalized Follow-ups:

Using data on customer communication preferences and past interactions, sales reps can tailor their follow-up strategies.

Example: Alex, who rarely answers phone calls but responds quickly to text messages, receives a follow-up text with additional information about the vehicle he is interested in.

Importance of CRM Training

While having access to customer data is crucial, its effectiveness hinges on the ability of sales staff to utilize this information effectively. Comprehensive training in Customer Relationship Management (CRM) systems is essential for several reasons:

1. Data Accuracy: Sales staff need to understand the importance of inputting accurate, complete data into the CRM system. This ensures that future interactions and analyses are based on reliable information.

2. Privacy Compliance: With regulations like GDPR and CCPA, it's crucial that sales staff understand how to handle customer data in compliance with privacy laws.

3. Effective Data Interpretation: Training should focus on how to interpret the data provided by the CRM system and translate it into actionable sales strategies.

4. Consistent Customer Experience: When all staff members are proficient in using the CRM system, it ensures a consistent, high-quality experience for customers across all touchpoints.

5. Continuous Improvement: Regular training sessions can introduce new features or best practices, ensuring that the sales team is always utilizing the CRM system to its full potential.

Case Study: *AutoNation's Digital Sales Assistant*

AutoNation, America's largest automotive retailer, implemented a digital sales assistant tool integrated with their CRM system. This tool provides sales representatives with real-time customer information and personalized talking points.

Results:

- 20% increase in lead conversion rates
- 15% improvement in customer satisfaction scores
- 10% reduction in the average time to close a sale

The success of this initiative was largely attributed to comprehensive staff training, which ensured that sales representatives were comfortable using the tool and could seamlessly incorporate data-driven insights into their sales approach.

Identifying the Most Effective Sales Tactics

In the data-driven era, dealerships no longer need to rely on gut feelings or outdated assumptions about what sales tactics work best. By analyzing sales data, they can identify the most effective strategies and continuously refine their approach.

Sales Data Analysis

1. Conversion Rate Analysis: By examining which sales tactics lead to the highest conversion rates, dealerships can focus their efforts on the most effective strategies.

Example: Data analysis reveals that customers who take an extended test drive (over 30 minutes) are 40% more likely to make a purchase. The dealership has adjusted its policy to encourage longer test drives.

2. Time-to-Sale Analysis: Understanding how different tactics affect the time it takes to close a sale can help optimize the sales process.

Example: Analysis shows that providing a detailed vehicle history report upfront reduces the average time-to-sale by 20%. The dealership implements a policy to provide these reports proactively.

3. Upsell Success Rates: Analyzing which add-ons or upgrades are most successfully sold can inform sales training and inventory decisions.

Example: Data reveals that customers buying SUVs are most likely to add roof racks and all-weather floor mats. Sales staff are trained to highlight these options for SUV buyers.

4. Promotional Offer Effectiveness: By analyzing the success rates of different promotional offers, dealerships can optimize their marketing strategies.

Example: Data shows that "0% financing for 60 months" is more effective in driving sales than "$2000 cash back" for luxury vehicles. The dealership adjusts its promotional strategy accordingly.

A/B Testing in Sales Strategies

A/B testing, a method of comparing two versions of a sales approach to determine which performs better, can be a powerful tool for continuously refining sales strategies.

1. Email Subject Lines: Test different subject lines to see which leads to higher open rates and engagement.

Example: "Your dream car awaits" vs. "Exclusive offer inside" - the subject line with the higher open rate is adopted for future campaigns.

2. Call-to-Action Phrases: Compare different CTA phrases on the website or in marketing materials to see which generates more leads.

Example: "Schedule a test drive" vs. "Experience it yourself" - the phrase that generates more clicks is implemented across all platforms.

3. Pricing Presentation: Test different ways of presenting pricing information to see which leads to higher conversion rates.

Example: Presenting the total price upfront vs. focusing on monthly payments - the method that results in more sales is adopted as the standard approach.

4. Follow-up Timing: Test different timings for follow-up contacts to determine the optimal window for re-engaging potential customers.

Example: Following up after two days vs. five days - the timing that results in higher engagement becomes the new standard practice.

Case Study: *CarMax's Data-Driven Sales Approach*

CarMax, the largest used-car retailer in the United States, implemented a data-driven approach to optimize its sales tactics. They used advanced analytics to analyze millions of customer interactions and transactions.

Key findings and implementations:

- ✓ Discovered that customers who received a personalized follow-up email within 24 hours of their visit were 35% more likely to return. Implemented an automated system to ensure timely follow-ups.
- ✓ Found that customers were more likely to make a purchase when given the option to "hold" a vehicle for 24 hours. Introduced a 24-hour hold policy.
- ✓ Identified that customers who used the online car appraisal tool before visiting were 20% more likely to make a purchase. Increased promotion of this tool across marketing channels.

Results:

- ✓ 15% increase in overall conversion rate
- ✓ 10% reduction in average time-to-sale
- ✓ 25% improvement in customer satisfaction scores

Automating and Optimizing the Sales Funnel Using Data-Driven Insights

In today's digital-first world, much of the car buying process happens before a customer ever sets foot in a dealership. Automating and optimizing the sales funnel can help dealerships guide potential customers through their journey more effectively.

Use of Automation Tools

1. Chatbots: Implement AI-powered chatbots on the dealership website to answer common questions and guide customers to relevant information 24/7.

Example: A chatbot can help customers narrow down their vehicle choices based on their preferences, schedule test drives, or provide instant answers about financing options.

2. Email Drip Campaigns: Set up automated email sequences that provide relevant information to potential customers based on their interests and stage in the buying journey.

Example: A customer who showed interest in electric vehicles receives a series of emails over several weeks, each highlighting different aspects of EV ownership (range, charging infrastructure, environmental benefits, etc.).

3. Retargeting Ads: Use data on customer website behavior to serve targeted ads across other websites and social media platforms.

Example: A customer who viewed SUVs on the dealership website sees ads for similar SUVs when browsing other websites or social media.

4. Automated Appointment Scheduling: Implement systems that allow customers to schedule test drives or consultations online, with automated reminders and follow-ups.

Example: After scheduling a test drive online, the customer receives an automated confirmation email, a reminder text message the day before, and a follow-up email after the appointment.

5. Virtual Reality Showrooms: Utilize VR technology to allow customers to explore vehicles from the comfort of their homes, with data on their interactions informing follow-up strategies.

Example: A customer who spent significant time examining the interior features of a particular model in the VR showroom receives follow-up information highlighting those specific features.

Lead Scoring and Machine Learning

Lead scoring is the process of assigning values to each lead based on various attributes and behaviors, allowing sales teams to prioritize their efforts on the most promising prospects. Machine learning can significantly enhance the accuracy and effectiveness of lead scoring.

1. Behavioral Scoring: Assign points based on customer actions, such as website visits, email opens, content downloads, etc.

Example: A customer who has visited the pricing page multiple times, downloaded a vehicle brochure, and opened several promotional emails would receive a high behavioral score.

2. Demographic Scoring: Assign points based on how well a lead's demographics match the ideal customer profile.

Example: If data shows that married individuals aged 35-50 with a household income over $100,000 are most likely to purchase luxury vehicles, leads matching this profile would receive higher demographic scores.

3. Engagement Scoring: Assign points based on a lead's level of engagement with the dealership across various channels.

Example: A lead who has interacted with the dealership on social media, responded to emails, and visited the showroom would receive a high engagement score.

4. Predictive Scoring: Use machine learning algorithms to analyze historical data and predict the likelihood of a lead converting.

Example: The system analyzes patterns from past sales data and applies these insights to new leads, assigning a predictive score based on the probability of conversion.

5. Dynamic Scoring: Implement machine learning models that continuously update scores based on new data and changing market conditions.

Example: If the model detects a shift in buying patterns (e.g., increased interest in electric vehicles following a spike in gas prices), it adjusts scoring criteria accordingly.

Case Study: Tesla's Data-Driven Direct Sales Model

While Tesla's direct sales model differs from traditional dealerships, their use of data and automation in the sales process offers valuable insights:

- ➢ Implemented a fully online ordering system, allowing customers to configure and purchase vehicles entirely online.
- ➢ Used data on customer configurations to inform inventory decisions and production priorities.
- ➢ Implemented a virtual assistant to guide customers through the configuration process, offering suggestions based on preferences and usage patterns.
- ➢ Utilized predictive analytics to forecast demand and optimize delivery schedules.

Results:

- ✓ Reduced average time from order to delivery by 30%
- ✓ Increased customer satisfaction scores by 25%
- ✓ Achieved a remarkably low inventory turnover time, often building cars to order

Challenges and Considerations

While the benefits of data-driven sales processes are clear, there are challenges that dealerships must navigate:

1. Data Privacy: Ensuring compliance with data protection regulations and maintaining customer trust is crucial.

2. Technology Adoption: Some customers may prefer traditional sales approaches, necessitating a balanced approach that caters to various preferences.

3. Human Touch: While automation can enhance efficiency, it's important to maintain the personal connection that many customers value in the car buying process.

4. Data Quality: The effectiveness of data-driven strategies relies on the accuracy and completeness of the data collected.

5. Continuous Learning: The automotive market is constantly evolving, requiring ongoing adjustments to sales strategies and continuous training for sales staff.

The integration of big data and advanced analytics into the automotive sales process represents a paradigm shift in how cars are sold. By leveraging customer data to personalize the sales experience, identifying the most effective sales tactics through rigorous analysis, and automating key aspects of the sales funnel, dealerships can significantly enhance their effectiveness and improve customer satisfaction.

However, it's important to remember that while data and technology are powerful tools, the human element remains crucial in the car buying process. The most successful dealerships will be those that can strike the right balance between data-driven insights and the personal touch that many customers still value.

As we move forward, the role of data in shaping sales strategies will only grow more significant. Dealerships that can effectively harness these technologies while maintaining a focus on customer relationships will be well-positioned to thrive in the increasingly competitive automotive retail landscape.

In the next chapter, we will explore how big data is transforming after-sales service and customer retention strategies in the automotive industry, examining how dealerships can use data to enhance the ownership experience and build long-term customer loyalty.

Chapter 5

Improving Customer Retention and Loyalty

In the competitive landscape of automotive retail, acquiring a new customer is just the beginning. The real challenge—and often the key to long-term profitability—lies in retaining customers and fostering loyalty. In this data-driven era, dealerships have unprecedented opportunities to understand their customers deeply, predict their behavior, and craft strategies that keep them coming back. This chapter explores how big data and advanced analytics can be leveraged to enhance customer retention and build lasting loyalty.

Analyzing Customer Lifetime Value and Identifying High-Value Customers

Customer Lifetime Value (CLV) is a metric that predicts the total value a customer will bring to a business over the entire course of their relationship. In the automotive industry, where a single customer might purchase multiple vehicles over their lifetime and generate significant service revenue, understanding and maximizing CLV is crucial.

Techniques for Calculating Customer Lifetime Value

1. Basic CLV Calculation:

CLV = (Average Purchase Value × Number of Purchases) × Average Customer Lifespan

This simple formula provides a starting point, but in the automotive industry, we need to consider additional factors:

2. Enhanced Automotive CLV Calculation:

CLV = (Vehicle Purchase Value + Service Revenue + Referral Value - Customer Acquisition Cost) × Expected Relationship Duration

Let's break this down:

- ❖ Vehicle Purchase Value: The profit margin on vehicle sales.
- ❖ Service Revenue: Income from maintenance, repairs, and parts over the customer's lifetime.
- ❖ Referral Value: The value of new customers brought in through referrals.
- ❖ Customer Acquisition Cost: The cost of marketing and sales efforts to acquire the customer.
- ❖ Expected Relationship Duration: The predicted length of the customer relationship, often based on historical data and predictive modeling.

3. Predictive CLV Modeling:

More advanced techniques use machine learning algorithms to predict future customer behavior based on historical data. These models might consider factors such as:

- ❖ Customer demographics
- ❖ Purchase history
- ❖ Service intervals
- ❖ Interaction frequency
- ❖ Economic indicators
- ❖ Vehicle depreciation rates

Example: A dealership uses a machine learning model that considers a customer's age, income, previous purchase history, and service record to predict their likelihood of purchasing another vehicle within the next five years and their expected service revenue during that period.

Strategies for Segmenting Customers Based on CLV

Once CLV is calculated, customers can be segmented to tailor retention strategies:

1. High CLV / High Loyalty: These are the most valuable customers. Focus on maintaining their loyalty through personalized service and exclusive offers.

2. High CLV / Low Loyalty: These customers have high potential but are at risk of churning. Prioritize retention efforts for this group.

3. Low CLV / High Loyalty: While not the highest value, these customers are stable. Look for opportunities to increase their value through upselling and cross-selling.

4. Low CLV / Low Loyalty: These customers require evaluation. Some may have potential for growth, while others might not be worth extensive retention efforts.

Strategies for Targeting High-Value Customers

1. VIP Service Programs: Offer priority scheduling for service appointments, loaner vehicles, and dedicated support lines to high CLV customers.

Example: "AutoElite" program that provides members with complimentary annual detailing, priority service scheduling, and exclusive event invitations.

2. Personalized Upgrade Offers: Use data on vehicle age, mileage, and market conditions to present timely, personalized upgrade offers.

Example: A system that automatically generates personalized emails to high CLV customers when their vehicle reaches five years or 60,000 miles, showcasing new models that align with their preferences.

3. Exclusive Access: Provide early access to new models or limited editions to make high-value customers feel special.

Example: Invitation-only preview events for upcoming luxury vehicle launches, exclusively for top-tier CLV customers.

4. Tailored Financial Products: Develop financing or leasing options specifically for loyal, high-value customers.

Example: A loyalty lease program offering reduced rates and flexible terms for customers on their third consecutive lease.

5. Referral Incentives: Implement a tiered referral program with increasingly valuable rewards for high CLV customers.

Example: A program where customers receive increasing benefits (from service credits to vacation packages) based on the number and value of successful referrals.

Case Study: *Lexus' Tiered Loyalty Program*

Lexus, Toyota's luxury vehicle division, implemented a data-driven, tiered loyalty program called "Lexus Elite Rewards." The program uses CLV calculations and customer behavior data to place customers into different tiers, each with its own set of benefits.

Key features:

- ✓ Points system based on vehicle purchases, service visits, and referrals
- ✓ Tiers ranging from "Select" to "Elite" with increasing benefits
- ✓ Personalized offers based on customer preferences and vehicle history
- ✓ Exclusive events and early access to new models for top-tier members

Results:

- 25% increase in service visit frequency among program members
- 15% higher repurchase rate for program members compared to non-members
- 30% increase in referrals from top-tier members

Developing Targeted Retention Strategies Based on Customer Behavior

Understanding why customers churn is crucial for developing effective retention strategies. Data analytics can provide deep insights into customer behavior and help predict and prevent churn.

Using Data Analytics to Understand Customer Churn

1. Churn Prediction Models: Develop machine learning models that predict the likelihood of a customer leaving based on various factors:

- Time since last purchase or service visit
- Frequency and nature of customer complaints
- Changes in service visit patterns
- Interactions with competitors (e.g., test drives at other dealerships)
- Life events (e.g., moving, changes in family size)

Example: A model identifies that customers who haven't had a service visit in 18 months and have recently moved to a new area are at high risk of churning.

2. Sentiment Analysis: Use natural language processing to analyze customer feedback from surveys, social media, and customer service interactions to identify dissatisfaction early.

Example: An AI system flags a pattern of negative sentiment in social media posts from customers about a particular vehicle model's fuel efficiency, allowing the dealership to proactively address concerns.

3. Behavioral Segmentation: Group customers based on their interaction patterns and preferences to tailor retention strategies.

Example: Identify customers who primarily interact online and develop digital-first retention strategies for this segment.

4. Lifecycle Analysis: Understand at what points in the customer lifecycle churn is most likely to occur and why.

Example: Data shows that customers are most likely to switch brands 6-12 months before their lease expires. The dealership implements a program of targeted communications and offers during this critical period.

Case Examples of Effective Retention Campaigns and Loyalty Programs

1. BMW's "Ultimate Service" Program:

BMW used data analytics to identify that maintenance costs were a significant factor in customer churn. They implemented a program offering free scheduled maintenance for the first four years or 50,000 miles.

Results:

- 20% increase in customer retention
- 15% increase in service department revenue from additional services and repairs

2. Tesla's Over-the-Air Updates:

Tesla leveraged its connected car technology to provide regular software updates that add new features and improve performance, creating ongoing value for customers.

Results:

- 35% reduction in churn rate
- 25% increase in customer satisfaction scores

3. Ford's FordPass Rewards Program:

Ford implemented a points-based loyalty program that rewards customers for purchases, service visits, and even certain app-based activities.

Results:

- 30% increase in service visit frequency among program members
- 20% higher repurchase rate for program members

4. CarMax's "Love Your Car Guarantee":

CarMax used customer feedback data to identify that the fear of making the wrong choice was a significant barrier to purchasing and repurchasing. They implemented a 30-day money-back guarantee and a 24-hour test drive option.

Results:

- 25% reduction in return rates
- 15% increase in customer satisfaction scores
- 10% increase in repeat purchases

Leveraging Data to Enhance the Post-Sale Customer Experience

The customer relationship doesn't end at the point of sale. In fact, the post-sale experience is crucial for building long-term loyalty. Data can play a pivotal role in enhancing this experience.

Importance of Maintaining Customer Relationships

1. Personalized Follow-ups: Use data on customer preferences and behavior to tailor follow-up communications.

Example: A system that automatically generates personalized emails based on the customer's vehicle usage patterns, offering tips for maximizing fuel efficiency for high-mileage drivers or showcasing off-road features for customers who've engaged with adventure-related content.

2. Smart Service Reminders: Leverage connected car data to provide timely, relevant service reminders.

Example: An AI system that analyzes vehicle diagnostic data and driving patterns to predict when a service will be needed, sending a reminder to the customer with a suggested appointment time and any relevant promotional offers.

3. Intelligent Customer Satisfaction Surveys: Use data to optimize the timing and content of surveys.

Example: A system that sends a brief, targeted survey 48 hours after a service visit, with questions tailored based on the type of service performed and the customer's history.

4. Proactive Problem Resolution: Use data analytics to identify and address potential issues before they become major problems.

Example: An AI system that analyzes service records and customer complaints to identify emerging issues with specific vehicle models, allowing the dealership to proactively reach out to affected customers with solutions.

Customizing After-Sales Services

1. Predictive Maintenance: Use data from connected cars to predict when maintenance will be needed and offer convenient scheduling options.

Example: A system that detects when brake pads are wearing low and automatically sends the customer a notification with a link to schedule a replacement service.

2. Personalized Service Packages: Analyze customer data to offer tailored service packages that align with individual usage patterns and preferences.

Example: Offer a "City Driver" package with more frequent oil changes but less frequent tire rotations for customers whose data shows mostly short, urban trips.

3. Customized Accessories Recommendations: Use purchase history and vehicle usage data to suggest relevant accessories.

Example: Recommend roof racks and bike carriers to customers whose data indicates frequent weekend trips.

4. Tailored Extended Warranty Offers: Analyze vehicle usage patterns and service history to offer customized extended warranty options.

Example: Offer a high-mileage extended warranty to customers whose data shows above-average annual mileage.

5. Personalized Trade-In Offers: Use data on vehicle age, mileage, and market conditions to present timely, relevant trade-in offers.

Example: A system that automatically generates a personalized trade-in offer when a customer's vehicle reaches five years or 60,000 miles, showcasing new models that align with their current vehicle's usage patterns.

Case Study: *Hyundai's Data-Driven Retention Strategy*

Hyundai implemented a comprehensive data-driven retention strategy focused on enhancing the post-sale experience:

Key features:

- ✓ Personalized maintenance schedules based on individual driving patterns
- ✓ AI-powered chatbot for 24/7 customer support, with escalation to human agents for complex issues
- ✓ Tailored loyalty rewards program offering points for service visits, referrals, and engagement with the Hyundai app
- ✓ Proactive recall management system that prioritizes outreach based on vehicle usage patterns and customer preferences

Results:

- ❖ 30% increase in customer retention rate
- ❖ 25% improvement in customer satisfaction scores
- ❖ 20% increase in service department revenue
- ❖ 15% reduction in customer support costs due to efficient AI-powered triage

Challenges and Considerations

While leveraging data for customer retention offers immense potential, there are challenges to consider:

1. Data Privacy: Ensure all data collection and usage comply with regulations like GDPR and CCPA, and be transparent with customers about how their data is used.

2. Data Quality: The effectiveness of these strategies relies on accurate, up-to-date data. Implement robust data governance practices to ensure data quality.

3. Balancing Personalization and Privacy: While customers appreciate personalized experiences, overly intrusive tactics can backfire. Strike a balance that feels helpful rather than invasive.

4. Technology Integration: Implementing these data-driven strategies often requires integrating multiple systems (CRM, DMS, connected car platforms, etc.). Ensure seamless integration for a consistent customer experience.

5. Staff Training: Equip staff with the skills to use these data-driven insights effectively in their customer interactions.

6. Measuring ROI: Develop clear metrics to measure the success of retention initiatives, considering both short-term metrics (e.g., service visit frequency) and long-term outcomes (e.g., CLV).

In the automotive industry, where a single customer can represent significant lifetime value, effective retention strategies are crucial for long-term success. By leveraging big data and advanced analytics, dealerships can gain deep insights into customer behavior, predict and prevent churn, and create personalized experiences that foster loyalty.

From calculating and segmenting based on Customer Lifetime Value to developing targeted retention campaigns and enhancing the post-sale experience, data provides the foundation for a customer-centric approach that can significantly improve retention rates and drive profitability.

However, it's important to remember that while data provides powerful insights, the human element remains crucial. The most successful retention strategies will be those that use data to empower staff to build genuine, lasting relationships with customers.

As we move forward, the role of data in shaping customer retention strategies will only grow more significant. Dealerships that can effectively harness these technologies while maintaining a focus on customer relationships and privacy will be well-positioned to build a loyal customer base in an increasingly competitive automotive retail landscape.

In the next chapter, we will explore how big data is transforming the service and maintenance aspects of the automotive industry, examining how dealerships can use data to improve efficiency, predict maintenance needs, and enhance the overall service experience for customers.

Chapter 6

Predictive Analytics and the Future of Car Sales

As we stand on the cusp of a new era in automotive retail, predictive analytics emerges as a powerful tool that promises to reshape the industry. By harnessing the power of historical data, current trends, and advanced algorithms, dealerships can not only anticipate customer needs but also stay ahead of market shifts. This chapter explores how predictive analytics is paving the way for a more proactive, efficient, and customer-centric approach to car sales and how dealerships can prepare for the evolving landscape of automotive retail.

Applying Predictive Analytics to Anticipate Customer Needs and Preferences

The ability to anticipate customer needs and preferences before they even arise is the holy grail of retail. In the automotive industry, where purchase cycles are longer and decisions are more complex, this predictive capability can be a game-changer.

Introduction to Advanced Predictive Models

Predictive models in automotive sales typically fall into several categories:

1. Time Series Models: These models analyze historical sales data to identify patterns and forecast future sales. They're particularly useful for predicting seasonal trends and overall market demand.

Example: A dealership uses a time series model to predict that SUV sales will spike in the autumn months, allowing them to adjust their inventory accordingly.

2. Classification Models: These models categorize customers based on

their likelihood to take certain actions, such as making a purchase or requiring a specific type of service.

Example: A model classifies customers as "likely to purchase in the next six months" based on factors like their current vehicle age, recent online behavior, and financial profile.

3. Regression Models: These models help predict continuous values, such as the price a customer is likely to pay or the frequency of their service visits.

Example: A regression model predicts the optimal price point for a used car based on its features, condition, and current market trends.

4. Collaborative Filtering Models: These models make recommendations based on the preferences of similar customers.

Example: A system recommends a specific vehicle trim level to a customer based on the choices of other customers with similar demographic profiles and browsing histories.

5. Natural Language Processing (NLP) Models: These models analyze text data from sources like customer reviews, social media posts, and service comments to predict sentiment and identify emerging issues or preferences.

Example: An NLP model analyzes social media chatter to predict growing interest in electric vehicles among young urban professionals in a specific region.

Integrating External Data Sources

While internal data provides a solid foundation for predictive models, integrating external data sources can significantly enhance their accuracy and scope. Key external data sources include:

1. Economic Indicators: Factors like GDP growth, unemployment rates, and consumer confidence indices can provide context for overall market trends.

Example: A model incorporates local employment data to predict demand for luxury vehicles in specific regions.

2. Social Media Trends: Analyzing social media conversations can provide real-time insights into shifting consumer preferences and emerging issues.

Example: A sudden spike in social media discussions about a new electric vehicle model prompts a dealership to adjust its marketing strategy and inventory plans.

3. Weather Data: Weather patterns can influence both short-term sales tactics and long-term inventory planning.

Example: A dealership in a snowy region uses long-term weather forecasts to predict demand for all-wheel-drive vehicles.

4. Competitor Actions: Data on competitor pricing, promotions, and inventory can help dealerships position themselves more effectively.

Example: A system that monitors competitor websites alerts a dealership to a rival's new financing offer, allowing them to quickly develop a counter-strategy.

5. Regulatory Changes: Upcoming changes in emissions standards, tax incentives, or other regulations can significantly impact buying behavior.

Example: A predictive model incorporates data on upcoming changes to electric vehicle tax incentives to forecast shifts in EV demand.

6. Technological Advancements: News and patent filings related to automotive technology can provide early indicators of future trends.

Example: A model analyzes tech industry news and research papers to predict growing consumer interest in advanced driver assistance systems (ADAS).

Case Study: *Toyota's Predictive Buying Model*

Toyota developed a sophisticated predictive analytics system called "T-Seeker" to anticipate customer needs and preferences:

Key features:

- ✓ Integration of internal sales and service data with external economic indicators and social media trends
- ✓ Machine learning algorithms that continuously refine predictions based on new data
- ✓ Personalized recommendations for individual customers based on their unique profiles and behaviors

Results:

- ➢ 20% increase in lead conversion rates
- ➢ 15% improvement in customer satisfaction scores
- ➢ 10% reduction in inventory carrying costs due to more accurate demand forecasting

Identifying Emerging Trends and Opportunities in the Automotive Market

The automotive industry is undergoing rapid transformation, with trends like electrification, autonomous driving, and shared mobility reshaping the landscape. Predictive analytics can help dealerships not only adapt to these changes but also identify new opportunities they present.

Use of Trend Analysis Tools

1. Sentiment Analysis: Use NLP techniques to gauge public opinion on emerging technologies and identify shifts in consumer preferences.

Example: A tool that analyzes online reviews and social media posts detects growing frustration with range anxiety among electric vehicle owners, signaling an opportunity for dealerships to focus on educating customers about charging infrastructure.

2. Patent Analysis: Monitor patent filings and research publications to identify emerging technologies that could disrupt the market.

Example: A system that tracks automotive patents identifies a surge in filings related to solid-state batteries, indicating a potential leap forward in electric vehicle technology.

3. Sales Trend Decomposition: Break down sales trends into various components (seasonal patterns, long-term trends, cyclical fluctuations) to identify underlying shifts in the market.

Example: An analysis reveals that while overall sedan sales are declining, there's a growing niche market for high-performance electric sedans among young professionals.

4. Predictive Market Segmentation: Use clustering algorithms to identify emerging customer segments with distinct needs and preferences.

Example: A model identifies a growing segment of "eco-conscious families" who prioritize both sustainability and practicality in their vehicle choices.

5. Scenario Modeling: Develop multiple future scenarios based on different combinations of trends and assess their potential impact.

Example: A dealership models various scenarios for the adoption rate of autonomous vehicles to plan its long-term business strategy.

Strategic Considerations for Adapting to Trends

1. Flexible Inventory Management: Develop systems that allow for rapid

adjustments to inventory based on predicted trends.

Example: Implement a just-in-time inventory system that can quickly respond to shifts in demand for electric vehicles.

2. Skills Development: Invest in training programs to ensure staff are prepared for emerging technologies.

Example: Develop a comprehensive training program for sales and service staff on electric vehicle technology and maintenance.

3. Strategic Partnerships: Form alliances with technology companies or startups to stay ahead of emerging trends.

Example: Partner with a local tech startup to offer innovative connected car services to customers.

4. Customer Education Initiatives: Develop programs to educate customers about new technologies and address potential concerns.

Example: Create a virtual reality experience that allows customers to "test drive" autonomous vehicles and learn about their safety features.

5. Diversification of Revenue Streams: Explore new business models that align with emerging trends.

Example: Develop a subscription-based model that allows customers to switch between different electric vehicle models based on their changing needs.

Case Study: *Volkswagen's MOIA Mobility Services*

Volkswagen launched MOIA, a mobility services company, in response to the growing trend of shared mobility:

Key features:

- ✓ Use of predictive analytics to optimize ride-pooling services
- ✓ Integration with public transportation systems
- ✓ Focus on electric vehicles to align with sustainability trends

Results:

- ➤ Successfully launched in Hamburg and Hanover, with plans for expansion
- ➤ Reduced urban traffic congestion by 20% in pilot areas
- ➤ Positioned Volkswagen as a leader in the evolving mobility landscape

Preparing Car Dealerships for the Evolving Landscape of Car Sales

As the automotive retail landscape continues to evolve, dealerships must adapt to remain competitive. This involves not only embracing new technologies but also rethinking traditional business models and customer engagement strategies.

Recommendations for Technological Upgrades

1. Cloud-Based Dealer Management Systems: Implement modern, cloud-based systems that can easily integrate with various data sources and analytics tools.

Example: A cloud-based DMS that provides real-time inventory updates, customer insights, and predictive analytics dashboards accessible from any device.

2. Virtual and Augmented Reality Tools: Invest in VR/AR technologies to enhance the customer experience both in-store and online.

Example: A VR system that allows customers to configure and experience vehicles in different environments, even if the exact model isn't physically present at the dealership.

3. AI-Powered Chatbots and Virtual Assistants: Implement advanced conversational AI to provide 24/7 customer support and generate leads.

Example: An AI assistant that can answer complex questions about vehicle specifications, schedule test drives, and even initiate the sales process.

4. IoT-Enabled Dealerships: Use Internet of Things (IoT) devices to create smart dealerships that can track customer behavior and optimize operations.

Example: IoT sensors that track customer movements through the showroom, providing insights on which displays are most effective and how to optimize the layout.

5. Advanced Data Analytics Platforms: Invest in robust analytics platforms that can handle big data and provide actionable insights.

Example: A predictive analytics platform that integrates data from multiple sources to provide real-time insights on market trends, customer behavior, and inventory optimization.

Staff Training Programs

1. Data Literacy Training: Ensure all staff have a basic understanding of data analytics and how to interpret key metrics.

Example: A monthly "Data Deep Dive" workshop where staff learn about new analytics tools and how to apply data insights in their daily work.

2. Tech-Savvy Sales Techniques: Train sales staff on how to effectively use new technologies in the sales process.

Example: A training program on how to use AR tools to showcase vehicle features and conduct virtual test drives.

3. Continuous Learning Programs: Implement ongoing training initiatives to keep staff updated on emerging technologies and market trends.

Example: A partnership with a local university to offer staff online courses on electric vehicle technology, autonomous driving systems, and other emerging automotive technologies.

4. Customer Experience Focus: Train staff to provide a seamless, technology-enhanced customer experience that blends digital and physical touchpoints.

Example: Role-playing exercises that simulate various customer scenarios, from online inquiries to in-store visits, emphasizing a consistent omnichannel experience.

5. Adaptive Selling Techniques: Train sales staff to use predictive insights to tailor their approach to each customer's unique needs and preferences.

Example: A training program on how to interpret customer data profiles and adjust sales strategies accordingly.

Potential Impact of Future Innovations

1. Artificial Intelligence:

- Personalized AI assistants that guide customers through the entire car buying process
- AI-driven predictive maintenance systems that schedule service before issues occur
- Automated inventory management systems that optimize stock levels in real-time

2. Internet of Things (IoT):

- Connected cars that provide dealerships with real-time data on vehicle performance and usage patterns
- Smart dealerships that adjust lighting, temperature, and displays based on customer preferences
- IoT-enabled test drives that capture detailed data on customer driving behavior and preferences

3. Blockchain Technology:

- Transparent, tamper-proof vehicle history records
- Streamlined, secure financial transactions and smart contracts
- Decentralized vehicle-sharing platforms that could disrupt traditional ownership models

4. Advanced Robotics:

- Automated vehicle detailing and maintenance services
- Robotic assistants that can showcase vehicle features and answer customer questions
- Fully automated warehouses for parts and inventory management

5. 5G and Edge Computing:

- Ultra-fast, low-latency connections enabling real-time virtual reality experiences

- ✓ Enhanced vehicle-to-everything (V2X) communication capabilities
- ✓ Edge computing allows for more processing to be done on the vehicle itself, enabling new features and services

Case Study: *Carvana's Fully Digital Car Buying Experience*

Carvana, an online used car retailer, has leveraged technology to create a fully digital car buying experience:

Key features:

- ✓ AI-powered search and recommendation system
- ✓ 360-degree virtual vehicle tours
- ✓ Automated financing approval process
- ✓ Robotic vehicle vending machines for pickup

Results:

- ➢ Grew from startup to Fortune 500 company in under ten years
- ➢ Customer base increased by 45% year-over-year in 2021
- ➢ Set new standards for convenience and transparency in car buying

Challenges and Considerations

While the future of car sales is undoubtedly technology-driven, there are challenges that dealerships must navigate:

1. Data Privacy and Security: As dealerships collect and use more customer data, ensuring privacy and security becomes increasingly critical.

2. Balancing High-Tech and High-Touch: While technology can enhance the buying experience, many customers still value human interaction. Finding the right balance is key.

3. Rapid Technological Change: The pace of technological advancement can make it challenging to decide which innovations to invest in and when.

4. Changing Skill Requirements: As technology reshapes job roles, dealerships may face challenges in recruiting and retaining staff with the necessary skills.

5. Evolving Regulatory Landscape: As new technologies emerge, regulations around data use, autonomous vehicles, and other innovations may impact dealership operations.

The future of car sales is being shaped by predictive analytics, emerging technologies, and shifting consumer preferences. Dealerships that can effectively leverage these tools to anticipate customer needs, identify market opportunities, and create seamless, personalized experiences will be well-positioned to thrive in this evolving landscape.

However, success in this new era will require more than just technological investment. It will demand a fundamental shift in mindset, embracing data-driven decision-making, continuous learning, and a willingness to reimagine traditional business models.

As we look to the future, the most successful dealerships will be those that can blend the power of predictive analytics and emerging technologies with the human touch that has always been at the heart of the car buying experience. By doing so, they can create a new paradigm of automotive retail that is more efficient, more personalized, and more attuned to the needs of the modern consumer.

In the next and final chapter, we will summarize the key insights from this book and provide a roadmap for dealerships looking to implement these data-driven strategies in their operations. We'll also look ahead to the potential long-term impacts of these technologies on the automotive industry as a whole.

Chapter 7

Implementing a Data-Driven Culture

In today's rapidly evolving automotive retail landscape, car dealerships that harness the power of data to inform their decision-making processes gain a significant competitive advantage. This chapter explores the crucial steps and considerations involved in fostering a data-driven culture within a car dealership organization, addressing the challenges that may arise, and developing the necessary skills and infrastructure to leverage big data effectively.

Fostering a Data-Driven Mindset Within the Car Dealership Organization

The transition to a data-driven culture begins with instilling a mindset that values data-driven decision-making at all levels of the organization. This shift requires a multi-faceted approach that encompasses several key strategies:

1. Lead by Example: Leadership must champion the use of data in their own decision-making processes. When executives and managers consistently rely on data to inform their choices, it sets a powerful precedent for the rest of the organization.

2. Establish Clear Goals and Metrics: Define specific, measurable objectives that align with the dealership's overall strategy. By tying these goals to data-driven metrics, employees can more easily understand the impact of their actions and decisions.

3. Promote Data Literacy: Invest in training programs that enhance data literacy across all departments. This includes teaching employees how to interpret data, recognize patterns, and draw meaningful insights from various data sources.

4. Encourage Data Sharing: Create systems and processes that facilitate the sharing of data and insights across departments. This can help break down silos and foster a more collaborative approach to problem-solving.

5. Recognize and Reward Data-Driven Success: Implement incentive programs that acknowledge and reward employees who effectively use data to drive positive outcomes for the dealership.

6. Integrate Data into Daily Operations: Incorporate data analysis into regular meetings, reports, and decision-making processes. This helps normalize the use of data and reinforces its importance in day-to-day operations.

7. Promote a Culture of Experimentation: Encourage employees to use data to test hypotheses and experiment with new approaches. This fosters innovation and helps the organization adapt to changing market conditions.

Despite the clear benefits of a data-driven approach, dealerships may face several challenges when implementing this cultural shift:

1. Resistance to Change: Many employees may be comfortable with traditional decision-making methods and resist the adoption of new data-driven processes.

2. Data Quality and Accessibility Issues: Dealerships may struggle with inconsistent or siloed data, making it difficult to derive accurate insights.

3. Lack of Analytical Skills: Some employees may lack the necessary skills to effectively analyze and interpret data.

4. Technology Integration: Implementing new data analytics tools and systems can be complex and may disrupt existing workflows.

5. Privacy and Security Concerns: Dealerships must navigate the ethical and legal considerations surrounding data collection and usage, particularly concerning customer information.

To address these challenges, dealerships can:

1. Communicate the Benefits: Clearly articulate how data-driven decision-making can improve individual and organizational performance.

2. Provide Adequate Training and Support: Invest in comprehensive training programs and ongoing support to help employees develop the necessary skills and confidence to work with data.

3. Start Small and Scale: Begin with pilot projects that demonstrate the value of data-driven approaches before rolling out larger initiatives.

4. Address Data Quality Issues: Implement data governance policies and invest in data cleansing and integration tools to ensure data accuracy and accessibility.

5. Ensure Data Security and Privacy: Develop robust data security protocols and educate employees on best practices for handling sensitive information.

Overcoming Challenges and Resistance to Data-Driven Decision-Making

Resistance to change is a common hurdle when implementing a data-driven culture. Some common sources of resistance include:

1. Fear of Job Obsolescence: Employees may worry that increased reliance on data will make their experience and intuition less valuable.

2. Skepticism About Data Accuracy: Some may question the reliability or relevance of the data being used to make decisions.

3. Comfort with Status Quo: Long-standing employees may be reluctant to change processes that have "always worked" in the past.

4. Lack of Understanding: Employees may resist due to a lack of understanding about how data can improve their work as well as the dealership's performance.

To overcome these sources of resistance:

1. Address Concerns Openly: Create forums for employees to voice their concerns and provide clear, honest responses.

2. Demonstrate Early Wins: Showcase successful data-driven initiatives to build confidence in the new approach.

3. Provide Personalized Support: Offer one-on-one coaching and mentoring to help employees adapt to new data-driven processes.

4. Involve Employees in the Process: Engage staff in the selection and implementation of data tools and processes to increase buy-in.

The role of leadership in driving this change cannot be overstated. Leaders must:

1. Articulate a Clear Vision: Communicate how a data-driven approach aligns with the dealership's overall strategy and goals.

2. Allocate Resources: Invest in the necessary tools, training, and infrastructure to support the transition.

3. Model Data-Driven Behavior: Consistently use data in their own decision-making processes and encourage others to do the same.

4. Create Accountability: Establish clear expectations for data usage and hold employees accountable for meeting these standards.

5. Celebrate Successes: Recognize and reward individuals and teams that effectively leverage data to drive positive outcomes.

Developing the Necessary Skills and Infrastructure to Leverage Big Data

To effectively leverage big data, car dealerships need to develop a range of skills and invest in appropriate infrastructure. Key skills required include:

1. Data Analysis: The ability to examine large datasets, identify patterns, and draw meaningful insights.

2. Statistical Modeling: Understanding of statistical concepts and the ability to create predictive models.

3. Data Visualization: Skills in creating clear, compelling visual representations of data.

4. Database Management: Knowledge of how to organize, store, and retrieve large volumes of data efficiently.

5. Programming: Familiarity with languages commonly used in data analysis, such as Python or R.

6. Business Acumen: The ability to translate data insights into actionable business strategies.

To develop these skills within the organization:

1. Implement Comprehensive Training Programs: Offer both in-house and external training opportunities to develop data skills across all levels of the organization.

2. Partner with Educational Institutions: Collaborate with local colleges or universities to create tailored data science programs for the automotive retail industry.

3. Encourage Continuous Learning: Provide resources and incentives for employees to pursue ongoing education in data-related fields.

4. Create Cross-Functional Teams: Form teams that blend data specialists with domain experts to foster knowledge sharing and skill development.

In terms of infrastructure investments, dealerships should consider:

1. Data Storage and Processing Systems: Invest in robust systems capable of handling large volumes of data, such as cloud-based storage solutions or on-premises data centers.

2. Analytics Software: Implement powerful analytics tools that can process and visualize complex datasets.

3. Data Integration Platforms: Invest in solutions that can seamlessly integrate data from various sources across the dealership.

4. Cybersecurity Measures: Implement robust security protocols to protect sensitive data from breaches and unauthorized access.

5. Mobile Technologies: Ensure that data and analytics tools are accessible via mobile devices to support real-time decision-making on the sales floor.

By focusing on these areas of skill development and infrastructure investment, car dealerships can position themselves to fully leverage the power of big data in their operations.

Implementing a data-driven culture within a car dealership organization is a complex but rewarding process. It requires a concerted effort to foster the right mindset, overcome resistance, and develop the necessary skills and infrastructure. However, dealerships that successfully navigate this transition will be well-positioned to thrive in an increasingly competitive and data-rich automotive retail landscape.

Chapter 8

Case Studies and Best Practices

As the automotive retail industry continues to evolve, car dealerships that have successfully integrated big data into their operations are setting new standards for performance and customer satisfaction. This chapter examines real-world examples of dealerships leveraging big data, distills key lessons and best practices from their experiences, and provides a practical roadmap for other dealerships looking to embark on their own data-driven journey.

Showcasing Successful Case Studies of Car Dealerships Using Big Data

Case Study 1: *AutoTech Motors - Personalized Customer Experience*

AutoTech Motors, a multi-brand dealership in California, implemented a comprehensive big data strategy to enhance customer experience and boost sales. They integrated data from various touchpoints including their website, CRM system, and service department, to create detailed customer profiles.

Key Initiatives:

1. Predictive maintenance alerts based on vehicle usage data and service history.

2. Personalized marketing campaigns tailored to individual customer preferences and lifecycle stages.

3. Real-time inventory optimization using market demand data and customer search patterns.

Results:

- ✓ 30% increase in service department revenue
- ✓ 25% improvement in marketing campaign conversion rates

- ✓ 15% reduction in inventory carrying costs

Lessons Learned:

- ❖ Importance of data integration across all customer touchpoints
- ❖ Value of predictive analytics in both sales and service departments
- ❖ Need for ongoing staff training to effectively utilize new data tools

Case Study 2: *EuroLux Autos - Pricing Optimization*

EuroLux Autos, a luxury car dealership in Germany, implemented a dynamic pricing model using big data analytics to optimize their pricing strategy for both new and used vehicles.

Key Initiatives:

1. Real-time price adjustments based on market demand, competitor pricing, and inventory age.

2. Predictive analytics to forecast future market trends and adjust procurement strategies.

3. Personalized pricing offers for repeat customers based on their purchase history and preferences.

Results:

- ✓ 20% increase in profit margins on used car sales
- ✓ 10% reduction in average days to sell for new vehicles
- ✓ 15% improvement in customer satisfaction scores

Lessons Learned:

- ❖ Importance of real-time data for effective pricing strategies
- ❖ Value of combining internal data with external market data

❖ Need for transparency in communicating pricing strategy to customers

Case Study 3: *TechDrive Dealerships - Data-Driven Operations*

TechDrive Dealerships, a network of dealerships in Japan, implemented a comprehensive big data strategy to optimize their entire operations, from inventory management to human resources.

Key Initiatives:

1. Predictive analytics for inventory management, considering factors like seasonal demand and economic indicators.

2. Data-driven performance metrics for sales staff, providing personalized coaching and incentives.

3. Automated customer feedback analysis to identify areas for improvement in sales and service processes.

Results:

- ✓ 25% reduction in excess inventory
- ✓ 18% increase in sales team productivity
- ✓ 22% improvement in customer retention rates

Lessons Learned:

❖ Value of applying data analytics across all aspects of dealership operations
❖ Importance of change management in implementing data-driven processes
❖ Need for continuous refinement of data models and analytics tools

Highlighting Best Practices and Lessons Learned from Industry Leaders

Based on these case studies and insights from industry experts, several best practices emerge for dealerships looking to leverage big data:

1. Integrate Data Sources: Combine data from all available sources (sales, service, marketing, external market data) to create a comprehensive view of your business and customers.

2. Invest in Data Quality: Ensure data accuracy and consistency through regular audits and data cleansing processes.

3. Focus on Actionable Insights: Don't just collect data for its own sake; focus on deriving actionable insights that can drive tangible business improvements.

4. Embrace Predictive Analytics: Use historical data and machine learning algorithms to forecast trends and anticipate customer needs.

5. Prioritize Data Security: Implement robust security measures to protect sensitive customer and business data.

6. Foster a Data-Driven Culture: Encourage data-based decision-making at all levels of the organization through training and incentives.

7. Continuously Refine and Adapt: Regularly review and update your data strategy to ensure it remains aligned with business goals and market conditions.

8. Invest in User-Friendly Tools: Choose data analytics tools that are accessible to non-technical staff to encourage widespread adoption.

9. Balance Technology with Human Insight: While leveraging data, don't lose sight of the importance of human experience and intuition in the car sales process.

10. Maintain Transparency: Be open with customers about how their data is being used to improve their experience.

Providing a Roadmap for Car Dealerships to Implement Big Data Strategies

For dealerships looking to start their journey towards becoming data-driven, here's a step-by-step guide:

1. Assessment and Planning (1-2 months)

   - Evaluate current data capabilities and infrastructure

   - Define clear objectives for your big data initiative

   - Identify key stakeholders and form a data strategy team

   - Develop a high-level roadmap and budget

2. Data Infrastructure Setup (2-3 months)

   - Choose and implement appropriate data storage and processing systems

   - Integrate data from various sources (CRM, DMS, website, etc.)

   - Implement data governance policies and security measures

3. Analytics Capability Development (3-4 months)

   - Select and implement analytics tools

   - Provide training to key staff members

   - Start with pilot projects to demonstrate value

4. Full-Scale Implementation (4-6 months)

   - Roll out data-driven processes across all departments

   - Implement change management strategies to drive adoption

   - Establish data-driven KPIs and reporting mechanisms

5. Continuous Improvement (Ongoing)

- Regularly review and refine data strategies
- Stay updated on new technologies and best practices
- Foster a culture of continuous learning and improvement

Checklist of Key Actions:

☐ Conduct a data readiness assessment

☐ Define clear, measurable objectives for your big data initiative

☐ Secure leadership buy-in and necessary budget

☐ Implement robust data storage and processing infrastructure

☐ Integrate data from all relevant sources

☐ Establish data governance and security policies

☐ Provide comprehensive training to staff

☐ Start with pilot projects in key areas (e.g., inventory management, customer experience)

☐ Implement data-driven KPIs and reporting mechanisms

☐ Regularly review and refine your data strategy

☐ Foster a data-driven culture through ongoing education and incentives

By following this roadmap and implementing these best practices, car dealerships can successfully harness the power of big data to drive business growth, enhance customer satisfaction, and maintain a competitive edge in an increasingly data-driven automotive retail landscape.

Chapter 9

Summarizing the Key Benefits of Using Big Data in Car Sales

As we reach the end of our exploration into the world of big data in car sales, it's crucial to reflect on the transformative impact this technology has had on the automotive retail landscape. This final chapter summarizes the key benefits of leveraging big data, provides encouragement for dealerships to embrace these powerful tools, and offers a glimpse into the future of data-driven practices in the automotive industry.

Throughout this book, we've examined numerous ways in which big data is revolutionizing car sales. Let's review the main points:

1. Enhanced Customer Understanding: Big data allows dealerships to gain deep insights into customer preferences, behaviors, and needs, enabling more personalized and effective sales approaches.

2. Optimized Inventory Management: Data-driven forecasting and demand analysis help dealerships maintain optimal inventory levels, reducing costs and improving turnover rates.

3. Precision Marketing: Targeted marketing campaigns based on data analytics lead to higher conversion rates and more efficient use of marketing budgets.

4. Improved Pricing Strategies: Dynamic pricing models informed by real-time market data help maximize profitability while remaining competitive.

5. Streamlined Operations: Data-driven insights can optimize various aspects of dealership operations, from staffing to service department efficiency.

6. Predictive Maintenance: Leveraging vehicle usage data allows dealerships to offer proactive maintenance services, enhancing customer satisfaction and service revenue.

7. Better Decision Making: Access to comprehensive, real-time data empowers managers to make more informed decisions across all aspects of the business.

Industry leaders have seen tangible benefits from adopting big data strategies. Here are a few testimonials:

"Implementing big data analytics has transformed our business. We've seen a 20% increase in customer retention and a 15% boost in overall sales. The insights we've gained have allowed us to tailor our approach to each customer's needs." - Sarah Chen, CEO of AutoPrime Dealerships.

"Big data has revolutionized our inventory management. We've reduced our carrying costs by 25% while improving our ability to meet customer demand. It's been a game-changer for our bottom line." - Marcus Rodríguez, Operations Director at EuroMotors Group.

"The precision we've gained in our marketing efforts thanks to big data is remarkable. Our campaign ROI has improved by 30%, and we're reaching the right customers with the right messages at the right time." - Aisha Patel, CMO of TechDrive Auto Sales.

Encouraging Car Dealerships to Embrace the Power of Big Data

To dealerships still hesitant about diving into the world of big data, we offer these words of encouragement: The automotive retail landscape is evolving rapidly, and data-driven practices are no longer just a competitive advantage – they're becoming a necessity for survival and growth.

The initial investment in time, resources, and cultural change required to

implement a big data strategy may seem daunting. However, the potential returns in terms of improved efficiency, customer satisfaction, and profitability far outweigh the costs. Moreover, as we've seen from the case studies and testimonials in this book, dealerships of all sizes and types can successfully leverage big data to transform their operations.

Remember, embracing big data is not about replacing human intuition and experience – it's about enhancing these valuable assets with powerful, data-driven insights. The most successful dealerships will be those that find the right balance between technological capabilities and the personal touch that has always been at the heart of car sales.

It's also crucial to recognize that the journey towards becoming a data-driven organization is ongoing. The field of big data and analytics is continuously evolving, with new tools, techniques, and applications emerging regularly. Successful dealerships will foster a culture of continuous learning and adaptation, staying abreast of new developments and constantly refining their data strategies.

Outlining the Future of Big Data in the Automotive Industry

As we look to the future, several trends are likely to shape the role of big data in the automotive industry:

1. Artificial Intelligence and Machine Learning: AI and ML technologies will become more sophisticated, enabling even more accurate predictive models and automated decision-making processes.

2. Internet of Things (IoT) Integration: As vehicles become increasingly connected, the volume and variety of data available to dealerships will

grow exponentially, offering new insights and opportunities for service and sales.

3. Augmented and Virtual Reality: Data-driven AR and VR technologies will transform the car buying experience, allowing customers to visualize

and customize vehicles in immersive digital environments.

4. Blockchain for Data Security: Blockchain technology may be increasingly used to ensure the security and integrity of sensitive customer and vehicle data.

5. Edge Computing: Processing data closer to its source (e.g., in vehicles themselves) will enable faster, more efficient data analysis and real-time decision-making.

6. Predictive Analytics for Vehicle Lifecycle Management: Advanced analytics will allow dealerships to predict and manage the entire lifecycle of a vehicle, from initial sale through multiple owners.

7. Integration with Smart City Infrastructure: As smart cities develop, dealerships will have access to broader datasets about traffic patterns, urban planning, and transportation trends, informing inventory and marketing decisions.

These trends are likely to reshape car sales in the coming years in several ways:

1. Hyper-Personalization: The car buying experience will become increasingly tailored to individual preferences, with personalized recommendations, pricing, and services.

2. Predictive Sales Models: Dealerships will be able to anticipate when a customer is likely to be in the market for a new vehicle and proactively engage them with relevant offers.

3. Subscription and Flexible Ownership Models: Data-driven insights will enable new, flexible car ownership and usage models, potentially shifting the traditional sales paradigm.

4. Seamless Online-Offline Integration: The boundary between online and in-person car shopping will blur, with data enabling smooth transitions between digital and physical touchpoints.

5. Automated Inventory Optimization: AI-driven systems will autonomously manage inventory, making decisions about which vehicles to stock based on complex market analysis.

6. Predictive Maintenance and Service: Vehicles will increasingly self-diagnose issues and automatically schedule service appointments, creating new opportunities for dealership service departments.

The future of car sales is inextricably linked to the power of big data. Dealerships that embrace this technology, continually adapt to new developments and find innovative ways to leverage data-driven insights will be well-positioned to thrive in the evolving automotive retail landscape. The journey may be challenging, but the potential rewards – in terms of improved efficiency, customer satisfaction, and profitability – make it a path worth taking. As we move forward, the most successful dealerships will be those who view big data not just as a tool but as a fundamental part of their business strategy and culture.

About the Authors

Richie Bello

Richie Bello is a solution-driven software developer, trainer, and consultant with over 30 years of experience in developing solutions for various industries. He is the CEO of Clickable, a leading digital media platform that provides reporting on various industries' performance.

Richie is also the founder of ShopSmartAutos.com, an online publication that offers consumers and dealers a better experience.

Richie leverages his expertise in marketing, sales, and branding to create and deliver world-class customer experience as CEO, of White Dove Bird.

He sits on the board of PCS Central America, a nonprofit organization that supports education and health initiatives. Richie founded the Richie Bello Institute of Leadership and Management, a not-for-profit focused on supporting U. S. military veterans.

Richie is a published author of three Amazon best-selling books with a focus on sales training. He is a US trademark for education, training, and coaching.

For more information visit **ShopSmartAutos.com.**

Mike Lewis, "The Book Guy"

Mike Lewis has created and published over 1000 best-selling authors, published over a dozen of his own bestselling books, has 40+ years of experience in marketing, sales, speaking, and coaching, and previously owned and was CEO of a $100,000,000 company. Mike's passion is for turning the real-world experiences of successful entrepreneurs, CEOs, and seasoned business experts into best-selling printed books and positively impacting their lives.

"Successful organizations realize that offering a remarkable product with a great story is more important and more profitable than doing what everyone else is doing a bit better." Seth Godin

For more information contact C. Mike Lewis at 404-281-6552.

www.ingramcontent.com/pod-product-compliance
Lightning Source LLC
Chambersburg PA
CBHW071946210526
45479CB00002B/830